PLAY BY PLAY
SOFTBALL

Coach Fred Wroge and the following athletes were photographed for this book:
Tamara Anderson,
Molly Chirico,
Rachael Ekholm,
Kathryn Hafertepe,
Colleen Hinz,
Dupe Omoyayi,
Tripper Teslow,
Katie Wells,
Katie White,
Leah Zarn.

LERNER
SPORTS
A DIVISION OF LERNER PUBLISHING GROUP

PLAY BY PLAY
SOFTBALL

Kristin Wolden Nitz

Photographs by Andy King

Lerner Publications Company ● Minneapolis

To Kurt Nitz

Lerner Publications Company
A division of Lerner Publishing Group
241 First Avenue North
Minneapolis, MN 55401 U.S.A.

Website address: www.lernerbooks.com

Library of Congress Cataloging-in-Publication Data

Nitz, Kristin Wolden.
    Play by Play. Softball / Kristin Wolden Nitz ; photographs by Andy King.
        p. cm.
    Rev. ed. of: Fundamental softball. ©1997
    Includes bibliographical references and index.
    Summary: Introduces the history, equipment, skills, and strategies of softball.
    ISBN 0-8225-9875-2 (pbk. : alk. paper)
    1. Softball—Juvenile literature. [1. Softball.] I. Nitz, Kristin Wolden. Fundamental softball. II. King, Andy, ill. III. Title.
GV881.N58 2000
796.357'8—dc21   99-047671

Manufactured in the United States of America
2 3 4 5 6 7 – GPS – 06 05 04 03 02 01

Photo Acknowledgments
Photographs are reproduced with the permission of: p. 8, The Hennepin County Historical Society; pp. 9, 51, ALLSPORT/Jamie Squire; pp. 10, 16 (both) © Peter Ford; p. 11, Photo courtesy of Sports Vision 20/20.

Diagrams and artwork by Laura Westlund.

CONTENTS

Chapter 1

HOW THIS GAME GOT STARTED

Each summer, more than 42 million people head for softball fields around the country. Some play only at an occasional picnic, but about 4 million diehards play in at least six tournaments a year. The field of play ranges from backyards and parks to stadiums filled with cheering fans.

Historians trace the origin of softball back to Thanksgiving Day in 1887. A group of young men spent their holiday at Chicago's Farragut Boat Club, following the progress of the Harvard-Yale football game—one telegram at a time. Tension grew. Bets were made. Yale won.

In the celebration that followed, a happy Yale booster playfully threw a boxing glove at the Harvard group. A Harvard backer swung at the glove with a stick and sent it sailing back over the pitcher's head. That was enough for George Hancock, who had

7

been watching the horseplay. He suggested a game. He used the glove's laces to tie it into a lumpy sphere and then drew paths on the gym floor with chalk. In the chaotic hour that followed, the teams scored 80 runs between them.

George Hancock thought they were onto something. He offered to write down a set of rules and provide a ball that wouldn't break any windows if his friends would stop by the boathouse on Saturday nights. By the end of that winter, Indoor Base Ball was being played all over Chicago.

Hancock's game could be played either inside or out, but a Minnesota fireman named Lewis Rober gets the credit for moving the game outdoors. In 1895, he set up a field in the vacant lot outside his firehouse so that his men could get some exercise while waiting for an alarm.

Rober's game had several advantages over baseball. It could be played on a smaller field since the

Lewis Rober, a firefighter in Minnesota, refined the game of softball and took it outdoors.

ball couldn't travel as far. A full game could be completed in an hour instead of three. And that hour was packed with plenty of offense.

The game spread to other firehouses. Leagues were formed. Sometimes 3,000 spectators would attend the games. The competition grew so fierce that family members playing on different teams stopped speaking to each other during the season. The game became known as kitten ball, after Rober's first team—the Kittens.

Across the nation, different forms of the game evolved. Each region developed a set of rules and equipment requirements. The ball's size varied from 10 to 20 inches in circumference. The amusing, often insulting, names of the game ranged from mush ball to pumpkin ball.

During much of the nineteenth century, the only games considered proper for women were noncontact sports like croquet, tennis, and badminton. The squishy ball, shorter field, and nonviolent appearance of kitten ball gave women the chance to play the new game. But contrary to the hopes of some, women didn't trot gently around the bases. By 1926, when the term softball first began to be used, women were playing a highly competitive sport resembling the modern fast-paced game.

The Chicago World's Fair of 1933 hosted the first national softball

Dot Richardson played shortstop for the 1996 U.S. gold-medal softball team.

SOFTBALL SURGEON

Many athletes have to undergo arthroscopic surgery for injuries. The shortstop for the 1996 Olympic softball team knows how to perform the procedure.

Dot Richardson, a doctor, put medicine on hold a year to train fulltime for the 1996 Olympics in Atlanta. She had already played on three Pan Am Games teams and in three International Federation world championships. But she said there was something special about representing her country in the Olympics.

Dot started in baseball but switched to softball by the age of 10. She jumped directly into a women's softball league. Three years later, she became the youngest player to join the national Women's Major Fast Pitch League. She has won seven Golden Glove awards.

People of all ages all over the world play softball for fun and exercise.

tournament for both women and men. More than 350,000 people attended the playoffs over the course of three days. The spectators then took softball home with them. Interest in the game spread.

Leo Fischer, a reporter who organized and wrote about the world's fair tourney, helped to found the Amateur Softball Association (ASA) in the fall of the same year. The ASA set standards for rules and equipment.

Variations still abound. Some are officially recognized. Others are not. In Chicago, Windy City or cabbage ball is played with a 16-inch ball and without gloves. In Maine and Alaska, people play in the snow. In Idaho and

Washington, some teams take snow-ball one step further and strap on a pair of snowshoes. At the opposite extreme, Californians developed a variation for playing in the sand called Over the Line. OTL players don't use gloves, and they don't run the bases. These versions of the game are popular in their regions, but fast-pitch and slow-pitch softball dominate the game nationwide.

The best fast-pitch players can hurl the ball so that it crosses the plate with speeds above that of a Major League Baseball pitcher's fastball. They can put stuff on the ball so that it rises, drops, or curves as it approaches the plate. As in baseball, fast-pitch is a duel between the pitcher and the batter.

Slow-pitch is a true team game. Everybody hits. Everybody fields. The pitcher's job is to lob the ball across the plate. The defense makes the outs. Don't underestimate the difficulty in hitting a pitch with a high arc. Few things are more amusing to a slow-pitch player than watching a cocky fast-pitch player swing and miss the ball.

The ASA crowns national champions in fast-pitch and slow-pitch, but fast-pitch dominates international competition. Softball has been played at the international level since the 1960s. It became a medal sport at the 1996 Summer Olympics.

BEEP, BEEP

Beep Baseball is an ingenious adaptation of softball for visually impaired athletes. The ball has a circumference of 16 inches. It is pitched underhand. Sighted players pitch and catch for their teammates.

The pitcher shouts "Ready" as the pitch leaves the fingers and then "Ball" at the moment the batter should swing. A beeping telephone in the center of the ball helps the batter judge where the ball is.

Once a batter hits the ball, a scorekeeper hits a button that starts one of two 4-foot pylons buzzing. These bases are located along the first and third base lines. The batter will wait to hear which pylon is buzzing before running full speed in the direction of the sound.

Meanwhile, the fielders are listening for the beeping ball. If the batter can make it to the base before one of six fielders "captures" the ball, a run is scored. Otherwise, the runner is out.

Chapter 2

THE BASICS

Young players begin playing softball by hitting balls off of a tee. At the next level, the batter faces an adult pitcher. Then youngsters begin pitching to each other. Soon, the pitches get faster.

Some players continue to play on high school and college teams, while other players head into recreational leagues. The term "recreational" should not be confused with non-competitive. These players play with a high level of intensity even as they're having fun. There are professional leagues for men and women. And, there are senior leagues for those over 55 years old.

Each league and every level has its own special rules. But despite small differences in equipment and field size, the game is instantly recognizable as softball.

The pitching rubber

The batter's boxes on either side of home plate

FIELD OF PLAY

The field is a square or one of its angles, so it looks like a diamond, and that is what it's sometimes called.

Home plate, where the batter stands, is the base of the diamond. First base is to the right of home, second base is directly across from home, and third base is to the left. The bases are 55 to 65 feet apart, depending on the type of game. The **pitching rubber** lies 35 to 50 feet from home plate in a direct line between second base and home.

The raked dirt around the bases is called the infield. The grassy region beyond is the outfield. Foul lines run from the pointed back of home plate, along the outer edges of first and third base and out to the fence. A ball landing between those two lines is in fair territory. A ball that first hits the ground outside those lines is a **foul ball.** A ball that hits the ground in fair territory and rolls across the foul lines before reaching first or third base is also a foul ball.

The two rectangles on either side of home plate are the batter's boxes. The areas marked in chalk to the left of third base and the right of first base are coaching boxes. This is where the coaches stand when their team is batting.

Distances Table

Fast-pitch

Division	Distance between bases	Distance from pitcher's rubber to home plate
ages 10 and under	55'	35'
girls 12 and under	60'	35'
boys 12 and under	60'	40'
girls 18 and under	60'	40'
boys 18 and under	60'	46'
Adult women	60'	40'
Adult men	60'	46'

Slow-pitch

Division	Distance between bases	Distance from pitcher's rubber to home plate
ages 10 and under	55'	35'
girls 12 and under	60'	40'
girls 14 and under	65'	46'
girls 18 and under	65'	50'
boys 12 and under	60'	40'
boys 14 and under	65'	46'
boys 18 and under	65'	50'
Adult	65'	50'

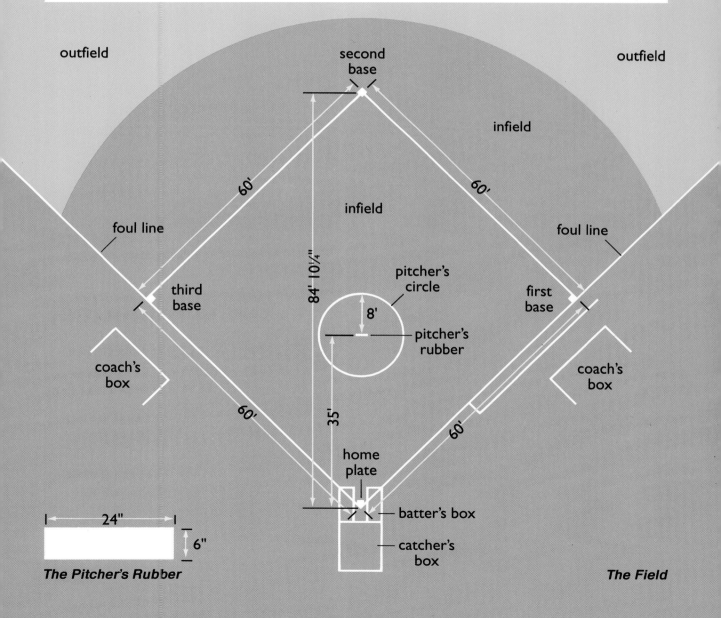

The Pitcher's Rubber

The Field

EQUIPMENT

The three parts of a softball are the core, the winding, and the cover.

Yarn is tightly wound around a cork, rubber, or fiber center. A 12-inch ball has a core measuring 3½ inches in diameter. The winding is about 1/16th of an inch thick. Cotton-polyester yarn is wrapped around the core and then is dipped into a special solution to hold the thread in place. The cowhide or synthetic cover is about 1/16th of an inch thick. It is cemented to the winding and hand stitched.

Twelve inches is the standard circumference for a softball. A 12-inch ball weighs 7 ounces, or just slightly more than a baseball. Balls come in many different sizes and colors. Youth leagues often use an 11-inch ball. Boxes of 16-inch balls are sent to Chicago for cabbage ball. The Over the Line players demand kapok balls with rubber covers. Kapok's silky fiber core becomes mushy during the game. Neon orange cork balls are used in the snow. Other "softies" are still made for the indoor game.

Because of their core construction and increased wind resistance, softballs don't fly as far as baseballs. That is why the distance from home plate to the outer fence is a little more than half that of a baseball park.

Make sure the pocket between the thumb and forefinger of your glove is large enough to catch the ball. Gloves actually improve with each season because the leather becomes more flexible with use. You can break in a glove faster by rubbing it with a conditioner. Between games and practices, many players leave a ball in the pocket and tie it shut.

Catchers use a different glove, called a mitt, above. It is bigger and doesn't have the individual finger spaces that a fielder's glove, below, does.

Batting helmets, at left, are hard plastic foam-lined hats that protect players while they're batting and running. Bats, at right, come in many sizes and colors.

Each bat has a handle, a barrel, and a knob. Players hold the bat on the taped handle and try to hit the ball with the thicker barrel. The knob helps to keep the bat from slipping out of the batter's hands. Bats are made of wood or aluminum.

A team's equipment bag will have a variety of bats. The bigger bats may carry nicknames like "Bleacher-reacher," but it's more important to pick a bat light enough to accelerate off your shoulder. The faster you swing, the more power you transfer to the ball. Grip the bat by the knob with your weaker arm. Hold the bat straight out in front of you. If the bat sags down, try a lighter bat.

Softball players usually wear loose, comfortable clothes to practice. Game uniforms vary from a T-shirt and shorts to a team jersey and short pants called knickers. Players never wear jewelry. Rings can be especially dangerous. A jammed finger can swell up so rapidly that a doctor must cut off the ring to restore circulation.

Special shoes with rubber cleats provide increased traction, but many people wear running shoes.

Batters and runners wear batting helmets to prevent head injuries. The catcher also wears a face mask, helmet, chest protector, and shin guards.

A catcher must wear protective gear in case he or she is hit by a ball or an incoming runner.

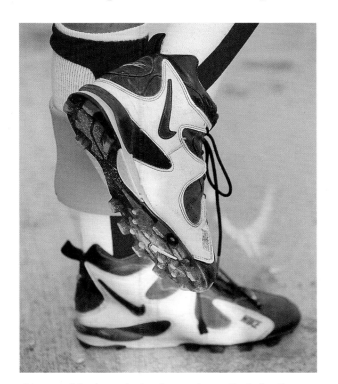

Shoes with cleats help players keep their footing on slippery outfield grass.

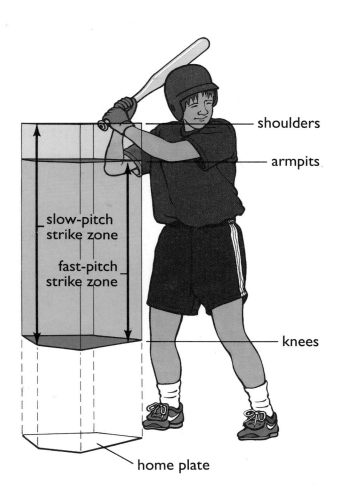

slow-pitch strike zone

fast-pitch strike zone

shoulders

armpits

knees

home plate

Strike Zones

THE RULES

The pitcher tries to throw the ball through the batter's strike zone using an underhand motion. In fast-pitch, the **strike zone** is the space over the plate that ranges from the batter's knees to the armpits. In slow-pitch, the zone goes up to the batter's shoulders.

If the batter doesn't swing at the pitch and the ball doesn't pass through the strike zone, the umpire will call a **ball.** The umpire will call a **strike** if the batter doesn't swing at a pitch that does go through the strike zone. A batter can also get a strike by swinging at the ball and missing, or by hitting a foul ball. If the **count** is already at two strikes, a foul ball isn't called a strike in most leagues.

A batter remains at the plate until he or she hits a ball into fair territory, takes four balls for a **walk,** or gets three strikes for an **out,** called a **strikeout.**

If the batter hits a fair ball, the defenders can make a **force-out** by throwing the ball to first base before the runner gets there. The runner is out if the defensive player has the ball and a foot on the bag.

If another runner is already on base, the defense will often choose to pick off the lead runner. If the lead runner doesn't have to run, a fielder must **tag** the runner to get an out.

For example, a runner on second doesn't have to go to third if there's no runner on first base. If the runner does go to third, the person playing third can tag him or her by holding the ball in the glove and touching the runner with it. The defense can also tag an offensive player who overruns second or third base.

The defense can also put the batter out by catching a fair or foul ball before it hits the ground. When that happens, all runners on base must **tag up,** that is they must be touching their original base until the ball is caught. When a **fly ball** is hit deep into the outfield, a runner may tag up and then run to the next base. Since the runner doesn't have to run, he or she must be tagged out. The offense scores a run when a person makes it all the way around the bases without being tagged or forced out.

Players bat according to the **batting order.** They cannot change places in this order but players can be substituted.

The visiting team bats first. This is called the top of the inning. The home team bats second, or in the bottom of the inning. Each team bats until the defense makes three outs. An inning is completed when both teams have batted.

Softball games last seven innings unless there is a tie or the game is rained out.

Chapter 3

FIELDING AND THROWING

Softball has many special strategies for playing the game effectively, but the mechanics can be broken down into two parts: stopping the ball and effectively sending it to the right place—otherwise known as fielding and throwing.

FIELDING

The secret to catching a fly ball is to watch it from the instant it leaves the bat until it smacks into the glove.

Sprint toward the area where you think the ball will come down. As you run, call out "I've got it." Say it over and over so that your teammates know that you will make the catch.

Even if you misjudge the ball and it winds up in someone else's territory, the catch is yours to make.

Catching a tennis ball with your bare hands is a good way to practice.

CATCHING THE BALL

There are two important principles to remember when catching the ball. First, you have to catch the ball before you can make the play. Basic? Yes, but countless players have bobbled the ball because they were thinking about making the tag instead of trapping the ball first.

Second, use two hands when catching the ball. That may sound like a rule for beginners, but it's not. Trapping the ball with your bare hand will keep it from ricocheting out. And with your hand already in position, you can quickly throw the ball.

DOING THE DIAMOND

The diamond drill can improve your speed, agility, and conditioning. Begin with your feet shoulder width apart. Jump so that your right foot lands at the top of the diamond while your left foot lands on the bottom. Return to the starting point, and then repeat the first motion except that your feet go to the opposite points of the diamond. Begin slowly and then go faster.

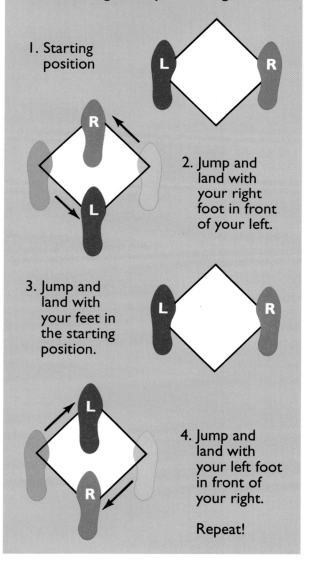

1. Starting position

2. Jump and land with your right foot in front of your left.

3. Jump and land with your feet in the starting position.

4. Jump and land with your left foot in front of your right.

Repeat!

Molly, below, shows how to catch a fly ball. She gets under the ball and holds her glove above her eyes with its fingers pointing up. This gives Molly a good view of the ball and shields her eyes from the sun. As the ball thuds into the pocket, she covers the ball with her other hand.

When a ball is driven deep into the outfield, Rachael, a smart outfielder, doesn't backpedal. She might trip over a rock or hole.

Instead, she turns and runs while watching the ball over her left shoulder. She catches the ball as she would a football pass.

It's important for a fielder to get under a fly ball. It's essential to get in front of a **ground ball.**

Since ground balls can be unpredictable, fielders must be ready to block the ball with their bodies. If the ball strikes a rock or an uneven piece of ground, it can take a bad hop.

As Tripper, at left, takes infield practice, he waits in the ready position. His feet are wide apart, his knees bent, his shoulders ahead of his hips, and his glove is down and open.

When a grounder bounces across the infield, Tripper moves in front of the ball. As he sets up to make the catch, the tip of his glove touches the ground so the ball won't roll through his legs. Tripper watches the ball until it enters his glove. Then he quickly traps the ball with his bare hand.

If the ball is rolling slowly, charge toward it, as Kathy does on the next page. Not only will she reach the ball faster, but also her throw will be shorter. The time saved in charging a ground ball can make the difference between a runner being safe or out.

Kathy gets in front of the ball to block it with her body. She knows if the ball gets past her, the runners will get extra bases. Like Tripper, she fixes her eye on the ball until it enters her glove and then covers the ball with her throwing hand.

OFF THE WALL

How can you work on your fielding by your-self? Throw a tennis ball against a wall or sturdy garage door. Change the angle, height, and speed of your throws to practice stopping many kinds of grounders.

A flat, hard-hit **line drive** doesn't leave a fielder much time to react. One of the toughest types to catch is a ball hit directly at the body.

In the photo at left, the line drive is above Kathy's waistline, so she catches the ball with her fingers and glove pointing up. In the photo below, she catches a zinger below the belt with her fingers pointing down.

On plays like this, things happen so fast that there isn't much time to think. That's why Kathy thinks through all of her options before the batter even steps up to the plate.

WARMUPS

Smart players don't just walk onto the field and start charging ground balls and throwing as hard as they can. To prevent injuries, they warm up first.

Begin by jogging around the outside of the softball field to loosen up and get extra blood flowing to your muscles. Then, do some stretching exercises. Remember:

1. Never stretch to the point of pain.
2. Breathe in and out normally.
3. Stretch both sides of the body equally.

Finally, warm up your throwing arm. Try playing catch on your knees. Not only is this a good way to warm up your arm, but it's also a good way to focus on the upper body motion.

THROWING

There are several different techniques for throwing the ball. Each one begins with a good grip.

Hold the ball with your fingertips, not in your palm. Try placing your middle finger and forefinger where the seams come together. Then hold your thumb underneath the ball to form an imaginary triangle passing through the softball.

Outfielders use the overhand throw to get the ball to the infield.

After Colleen, below, makes the catch, she faces her target and takes a short step forward with her ball-hand leg. As her glove-hand foot moves forward, her glove shoulder and hip point to her target. Her throwing arm is back, wrist cocked.

As her arm comes forward, her elbow passes her ear. Colleen shifts her weight forward to her glove-hand foot as she releases the ball and follows through.

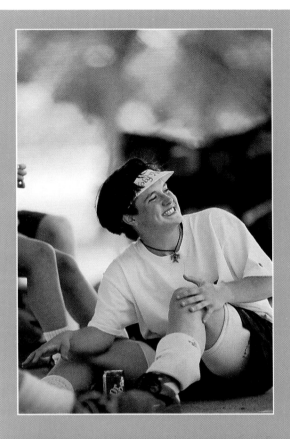

TEAM PLAYER

"What a team player!" That's a high compliment for a softball player, or any athlete. It means that player puts the team ahead of personal preferences or desires.

Being a team player can mean taking care of yourself so that you're always ready to play. That means eating right, getting enough rest, and stretching before you throw or practice.

Being a team player also means listening to your coach. Each coach does things in his or her own way. That means that what your coach did last year might not be what this year's coach does. A team player knows how to adjust to the coach's style.

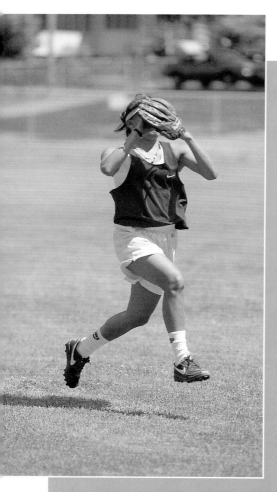

DOING THE CROW HOP

On a deep throw from the outfield, some players add an extra short step, called a crow hop. This move protects the arm and increases a player's throwing range.

Rachael demonstrates the crow hop. First, she fields the ball. Facing her target, she takes a short step forward with her ball-hand leg. Rachael hops on her ball-hand leg to add momentum. Her glove-hand shoulder and hip point to her target. She brings her throwing arm back with the wrist cocked.

As her arm comes forward, Rachael shifts her weight forward to her glove-hand foot as she releases the ball.

In addition to the overhand throw, infielders use the sidearm throw. The motion for the sidearm throw is similar to skipping a stone on a lake. Molly is making a sidearm throw in the photos on this page. Notice that Molly's forearm is parallel to the ground, and follows through across her body. This throw saves time since Molly doesn't have to bring her arm all the way back. Molly can also use this throw when she is off balance.

Snap throws are used in a run-down when a baserunner is trapped between bases. Below, Kathy's hand begins by her ear and ends with her arm at shoulder height and parallel to the ground.

A player can quickly deliver the ball from a crouch with an underhand throw. Since Dupe is only a few feet from the base, she gently tosses the ball so her teammate can catch it. She is careful that the ball doesn't

spin off her fingers and over her teammate's head.

Of course, the most important use for the underhand throw in softball is in pitching. The next chapter explains how to pitch.

Chapter 4

PITCHING

Good pitching takes concentration, control, and consistency. Successful pitchers coordinate their footwork with the release of the ball to develop a rhythm.

They also develop mental and emotional strength. They can't afford to get rattled after walking a batter or allowing a home run. Both slow- and fast-pitch pitchers need the same kind of mental toughness, but the rules of each game make the style of delivery very different.

In slow-pitch softball, the ball's arc must range from a minimum of 3 feet from the point of release to a maximum of 12 feet from the ground. A pitcher gets just one warning about excessive speed. After that, the umpire will remove the pitcher from the game.

In contrast, a fast-pitch ball can't have an arc of more than 3 feet. A pitch's speed in fast-pitch is limited only by the strength and skill of the pitcher and the laws of physics.

Pitching Arcs

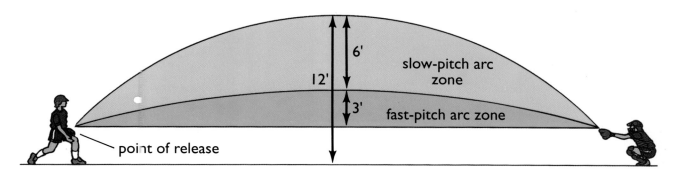

6'

12'

slow-pitch arc zone

3'

fast-pitch arc zone

point of release

SLOW-PITCH DELIVERY

Kathy begins with her ball-hand foot on the pitching rubber and her other foot back. She grips the ball with her fingers. She holds the ball behind her glove and in front of her chest for no less than two seconds. Then she swings her arm back gently until the ball is no more than hip high.

Kathy steps forward as she swings her arm forward and releases the ball just past her hip. She immediately jumps back and gets ready to field the hit.

The pitcher can keep the batter guessing by varying the arc and spin on the throw. With the proper arc, the ball can pass through the strike zone and hit the back of the plate for a strike.

PITCHING WARMUP

Whether you're practicing in your backyard or getting ready for a game, warm up your arm properly. Begin by running. Next, play catch, gently tossing the ball both underhand and overhand. This stretches muscles in your back, shoulder, and forearm.

When you begin your pitching warmup, make sure that you are the correct distance from your catcher. Start pitching at half speed and gradually accelerate until you are throwing as fast as you would throw to a batter. Do this for every type of pitch you will throw.

FAST-PITCH DELIVERY

There are two types of deliveries in fast-pitch: the slingshot and the windmill. Many pitchers master the slingshot first. For the slingshot, the pitcher's arm is drawn back slowly before it is whipped forward.

Pitchers can throw faster pitches with the windmill. This type of delivery got its name from old-fashioned trick pitches. Pitchers would rotate their arms several times to confuse the batter. Current rules allow only one revolution.

On the next three pages, Rachael demonstrates the slingshot. She begins with both feet touching the pitcher's rubber. Her ball-hand heel rests on top of the rubber while the toe of her other foot presses against the back of the rubber.

Rachael holds the ball with a two- or three-fingered grip. Her hands are down and in front of her body. She hides her grip in her glove for no less than one second.

Rachael brings the ball out of her glove. As she rotates her arm back, she steps forward with her glove-hand foot. By the time the ball reaches its highest point above and behind her head, her striding leg is fully extended. But Rachael keeps all of her weight back until she whips

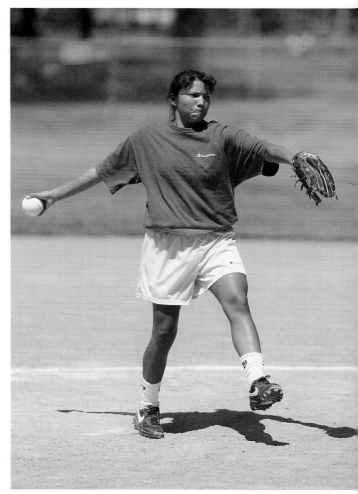

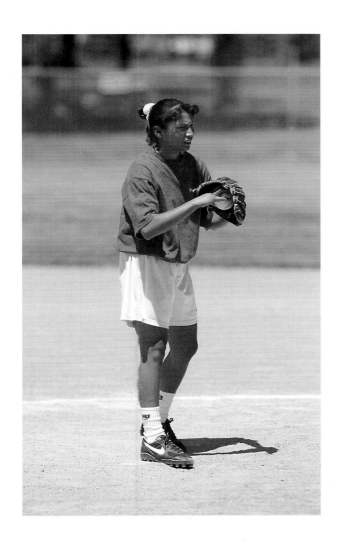

This side view shows how high Rachael brings the ball above her head during the slingshot.

her arm forward in a plane parallel to her body. She plants her foot an instant before she releases the ball.

Rachael snaps her wrist forward, adding speed and spin to the ball as it leaves her fingertips. Rachael's back foot leaves the mound an instant later.

After the release, Rachael's arm continues to rotate upward in a smooth motion. Since the ball could come straight back at her, Rachael instantly gets into fielding position. To do that, she makes sure that her striding foot hits the ground pointing directly at the batter.

To do the windmill, Leah brings the ball back and down out of her glove as if she were beginning the sling-shot. This motion stops at the hip and Leah begins to rotate her arm in

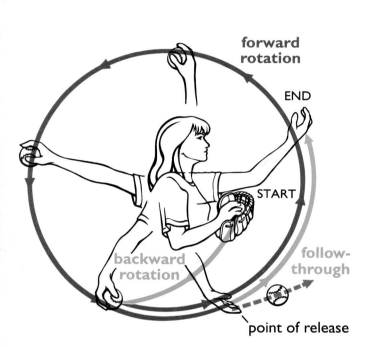

forward
rotation

END

START

backward
rotation

follow-
through

point of release

The Windmill Delivery

the other direction. She shifts her weight to her ball-side foot while beginning her stride.

As the ball reaches its highest point, Leah's leg is fully extended.

Once again, Leah keeps her weight back until passing this balance point to avoid throwing with just her arm. She snaps her wrist forward on the release as the ball passes her thigh. Her front foot hits the ground at the instant she releases the ball. Her back foot leaves the pitcher's rubber an instant later.

After the release, Leah's arm continues to rotate up in a smooth mo-tion. Then she quickly steps forward into fielding position.

Some pitchers add a pumping mo-tion to the windmill for better con-trol. They bring the ball and glove to their chest or face so that the grip is still hidden. As both arms head back to the original ready position, the ball hand leaves the glove. At that point, the arm starts forward and they use the usual windmill delivery.

This view from straight-ahead shows Leah releasing the ball just as her hand passes her thigh.

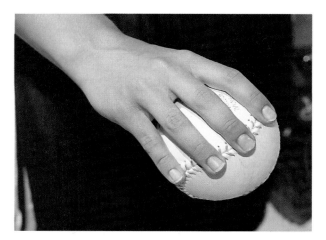

The drop ball grip

The rise ball grip

The curveball grip

STUFF

Different grips and ball rotations enable a pitcher to put stuff on the ball. Instead of traveling directly across the plate, these balls move sharply up, down, or to the side.

The most common pitches are the rise ball, drop ball, and curveball. A fourth pitch, called the changeup, is usually a slower drop or rise ball. The sudden decrease in speed and spin can fool hitters and make them swing ahead of the pitch. The key to a good change-of-pace pitch is to make the delivery look like every other pitch.

Several common grips are shown at left. For the drop ball, many pitchers use a two- or three-fingered grip. The fingers are placed evenly across the seams. The ball spins toward the batter and drops suddenly as it approaches the plate. The faster the pitch, the more sharply the ball will drop. Batters will often hit grounders when they swing at a drop ball.

For the rise ball, the middle finger is bent. As the hand passes the leg, the wrist rotates toward the body. This rotation causes the ball to roll off the fingertips with back spin. The curveball is delivered in much the same way as the rise ball, but on the follow-through, the arm should move across the body. Rising pitches often cause fly balls.

HOT STUFF

Lisa Fernandez, a pitcher on the 1996 gold medal-winning U.S. women's Olympic softball team, played her first game as a pitcher when she was eight years old. She walked 20 batters and her team lost the game 28–0. Instead of giving up, she decided that she would do better next time. She did.

Lisa continued to improve and ended her four years at the University of California at Los Angeles (UCLA) with a stunning record of 709 strikeouts, nine no-hitters, and three perfect games. She had an earned run average of 0.22. (An earned run occurs when the run is not the result of a defensive error, such as dropping a fly ball. To calculate an earned run average, divide the number of earned runs by the number of innings pitched, and multiply by seven.)

In Lisa's senior year, she had a .507 batting average, the best in the nation. She led the UCLA Bruins to four College World Series. They won the NCAA championship twice.

HITTING AND RUNNING

Everyone wants a turn at bat. There's nothing like connecting solidly with a pitch, beating a throw to first, or sliding under a tag. It's undeniably the most fun part of playing.

You and your teammates can transport yourselves to the league championship: *"Two outs in the bottom of the seventh. The score is tied with the go-ahead run on third. . . ."*

Just as with fielding, throwing, and pitching, it's important to learn the right techniques for hitting, running, and sliding.

HITTING

Hitting, like throwing and pitching, begins with the right grip. In the photo at right, Leah holds her hands together so that the hand knuckles of her top hand line up with the finger knuckles of her bottom hand. Some batters move their hands closer to the barrel, or choke up, on the bat for extra control as Leah has done in the photo to the far right.

On the left, Leah shows the regular way to grip a bat. On the right, she shows how to choke up on the bat. Players choke up when a pitcher is throwing very fast, the bat they're using is too heavy, or they want to have an exceptionally quick swing.

53

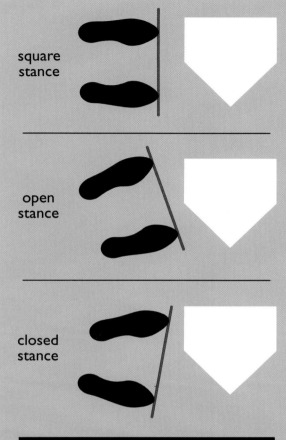

square
stance

open
stance

closed
stance

HIGH-POWERED FOOTWORK

Begin with your feet in the parallel, or square, stance with both toes pointed directly at the plate. Later, try the open stance where the front foot is farther away from the plate. Some batters prefer this stance because on an inside pitch, they can **pull the ball** down the foul line on the same side of the plate that they're standing on. Or, try to hit across to the **opposite field** by taking a closed stance in which the front foot is closer to the plate.

Slow-pitch players can change their stance while the ball is in the air. Fast-pitch batters don't have time to adjust once the ball leaves the pitcher's hand.

Leah stands in the batter's box with her feet about shoulder width apart and her knees flexed. She cocks the bat back behind her ear, halfway between the horizontal and the vertical. Her hands are even with her shoulders, and her arms are comfortably away from her body. She keeps her shoulders level and the bat off her shoulder.

Leah looks at the pitcher, resting her chin just above her front shoulder. Once the pitcher begins the delivery, Leah will focus on the ball.

As the pitcher delivers, Leah shifts her weight to her back foot. Her shoulders rotate back slightly. Her eyes are on the ball. Leah steps toward the pitcher with her front foot but does not shift her weight forward until she begins her forward swing. Leah's back hip follows the forward rotation of her hands, using her back foot as a pivot. She plants her front foot. Her arms are fully extended as she watches the ball down the barrel of the bat.

CURING POP UPS

Few things are more frustrating than popping the ball high above the infield. Pop ups have many causes. One possibility is that you are hitting under the ball instead of hitting it squarely. Check your stride. Some players have been cured of pop ups by taking a shorter stride and ending with their front leg straight rather than bent.

HITTING DRILLS

Hitting off a tee, as Colleen is doing above, can help your swing. Focus on one or two parts of your swing. For example, work on fully extending your arms and snapping your wrists. The next day, concentrate on your stride.

The soft toss drill Colleen and Dupe are doing below is another good one. Stand close to a fence and have a teammate gently toss a ball toward you. Swing hard and hit the ball into the fence.

Leah snaps her wrists as the bat contacts the ball. She rolls her wrists over as she swings hard "through" the ball. She ends with her front leg straight and her back leg bent. Her hands finish near her front shoulder.

To fully extend their arms and obtain maximum power, batters should connect with an inside pitch about three feet in front of the plate.

When the ball comes right down the middle, the bat should contact it two feet in front of the plate. This is called "hitting the ball where it's pitched."

Batters who know how to **bunt** can cause chaos. When the ball bounces off the bat, rolls a few feet from home plate, and stops, there's a moment of confusion as two or more people converge on the ball.

There's no bunting in slow-pitch. In fast-pitch, a bunt can be used when a batter is trying to make contact against a hard-throwing pitcher. Once the count reaches two strikes, many batters return to their normal swing since a foul bunt counts as the third strike.

The **sacrifice bunt** is one method of advancing a runner. It's known as a sacrifice because the batter will usually be thrown out at first base.

In the photos at right, Tripper demonstrates a sacrifice bunt. When the pitcher begins the windup, Tripper pivots to face the infield. The infielders are instantly alerted that Tripper intends to hit a sacrifice bunt. The fielders at first and third charge toward the plate.

Tripper slides his top hand along the bat with his fingers on the bottom and his thumb on the top. In this position, he can cushion the ball's impact while protecting his fingers. He adjusts to the height of the pitch with his legs. Instead of swinging, Tripper lets the ball hit the underside of the bat and directs the ball into the dirt.

The **drag bunt** is used when the batter wants to reach base safely. The drag bunt resembles the sacrifice bunt. The big difference is in the timing. Molly, above, acts as though she will swing, but shifts into the bunting stance while the ball is in the air. As she pushes the ball down one of the baselines, Molly is already on her way to first. That headstart can be the difference between getting on base and being thrown out.

RUNNING THE BASES

Intelligent, heads-up baserunning is important to the offense. Every player on base should know the count, the number of outs, and the score. All of these factors will dictate how aggressively a person can run the bases.

The runner should listen to the base coaches for information on whether to slide, come in standing up, or even try for another base. The base coaches will also deliver the signal to steal, using a series of gestures. Before the game, the coach may tell the team that a nose scratch means steal, a shoulder touch means stay, and a chin rub means run on a wild throw. All the other motions are used to make sure the other team doesn't guess the code.

At right, Dupe shows how to run to first. After hitting the ball, Dupe takes the first step with her back foot. Both right- and left-handed players should take off in that way from home plate. It's effective because the player's weight has been shifted to the front foot during the swing.

Dupe doesn't stop to watch the ball. She pumps her arms like a sprinter and runs straight across the bag. Since players can overrun first base, there's no point in slowing down or trying to slide into first.

DROPPED THIRD STRIKE

In fast-pitch, if the catcher drops the third strike, the runner can try to beat the throw to first base if:

1. First base is empty.
2. First base is occupied, but there are already two outs.

This rule prevents the catcher from dropping the third strike on purpose to get two outs. So don't give up on strike three!

On an **extra-base hit,** below, Dupe veers out in a slight arc as she runs to first base. As she approaches the bag, she turns toward second base and touches the inside corner of the base with her foot.

There isn't any stealing in slow-pitch because a runner could easily get to the next base as the pitch headed toward the plate. In fast-pitch, the baserunner can't lead off but the runner can leave a base as soon as the pitcher releases the ball.

Timing is critical to stealing a base. If you wait until you actually see the ball leave the pitcher's hand, you've already lost valuable time.

One trick, which Colleen demonstrates above, is to start with one foot behind the bag. As the pitcher reaches the highest point of the delivery, Colleen strides forward with her back leg.

Her foot stays on the base until the ball leaves the pitcher's hand. This helps Colleen get a good jump off the bag.

On a close play, you can slide to avoid being tagged. You can also slide to avoid overrunning a base.

Plan your slide well in advance and commit. Beginning a slide late or deciding not to slide after you begin the slide are two ways to get hurt.

The straight-in, or bent-leg, slide offers you the best chance to get right back up. Colleen demonstrates on these two pages. She begins her slide 10 to 12 feet from the base. She bends her knees to drop her hips and then extends one leg toward the bag while tucking the other leg under the opposite knee. She slides on the hip and upper part of the thigh and keeps her arms up in the air.

TAKING THE FIELD

The real excitement begins when you and your teammates face another team. Softball rules require that nine people take the field on defense. Six players play in the infield: pitcher, catcher, shortstop, first, second, and third base. The other three players cover their territory in the outfield either in rightfield, leftfield, or centerfield. Since slow-pitch softball is a hitter's game, some leagues allow a 10th player as a shortfielder in the outfield.

Standing alone at home plate, it's easy to feel outnumbered by the fielders. But the real battle is between you and the pitcher.

When you step into the batter's box, make the pitcher throw strikes. Don't swing at balls that whiz by your nose or skim over your shoelaces. Wait for your pitch. Keep your eye on the ball and try to make contact.

CONDUCT ON THE FIELD

When you play softball, show some class. Don't kick dirt or throw your glove, hat, or bat. Don't argue with the umpire. Ask your coach if you think there should be an appeal to the umpire.

Keep the chatter going continuously. Chatter lets everyone know the count and where to make the throw.

You can build up your teammates with phrases like "Nice pitch" and "Good throw." Or you can tease your opponents by yelling "Easy out" and "No batter." Just be prepared. Some players will respond to "She's afraid to take the bat off her shoulder!" by jacking the ball over the centerfielder's head. After all, that's what you're going to do, right?

65

PITCHER

A complete pitcher does more than face batters. Once a pitcher releases the ball, the job description changes. The pitcher becomes an infielder. One important task is to back up the catcher on a play at home. Depending on the number of runners and where they are, the pitcher may also back up a throw to second or third base. An added responsibility for the pitcher in fast-pitch is covering the plate if a pitch gets away from the catcher. An aggressive baserunner on third base might try to steal home.

CATCHER

Catchers need to be quick, tough, and flexible. They have to be ready for pop flies, finger-stinging foul tips, and runners barreling down the third base line on the tag play.

Catchers lead the defense. They study the opposing batters for strengths and weaknesses. They take charge of the chatter and make sure everyone knows the count and number of outs. Experienced catchers will know when and how to take their pitcher aside for an encouraging word. They also know when it's time for their pitcher to be replaced.

Fast-pitch catchers decide which pitch should be thrown. To signal the pitcher, Katie squats with her thighs resting on her calves, as in the bottom left photo. She points her fingers toward the dirt to send the signals. Then she holds up her mitt to give the pitcher a target. She puts her bare hand behind her back to protect it.

Once a runner makes it onto the base paths, the catcher watches for the steal. After giving the sign, the catcher moves from the squat to the up position. The catcher's legs are bent at the knee almost as though he or she were sitting in a chair. The catcher bends forward and extends the mitt.

When a runner is on base, the catcher's most important job is to make sure the ball doesn't get past him or her. If the pitcher throws the ball in the dirt, the catcher must block the ball by falling to the knees and putting the tip of the glove in the dirt. The catcher should lean forward so the ball doesn't bounce over a shoulder.

FIRST BASE

Like Tamara, the person playing first is frequently tall. Those added inches help when catching a high, wild throw. Tamara, above, is playing in front of the base, near the baseline, to defend against the bunt.

On a well-thrown ball, Tamara places her bare-hand foot on the corner of the bag. She stretches as far as possible to reduce the distance that the ball needs to travel. She must catch the ball so a single doesn't turn into a double. When a throw from the shortstop is in the dirt, she puts the tip of her glove close to the ground so the ball won't roll under it.

In the photos on this page, Molly is the shortstop. When the batter hits a pop fly in Molly's direction, she calls out that she'll catch it. Then she runs to get underneath the ball while the leftfielder backs up the play.

SECOND BASE AND SHORTSTOP

The infielders at second base and shortstop need superior fielding abilities and accurate throwing arms. Plays made at second base can decide a game. After all, once a runner reaches second base, that runner is in **scoring position.** The players standing to either side of second base must work closely together and know who is going to cover the base on every possible play

When the ball is hit toward the rightfield side of second, the shortstop will cover the base while the fielder at second plays the ball. If the ball is hit to the left of second, the fielder at second goes to the base and the shortstop fields the ball.

THIRD BASE

The third base position sees the greatest variety of balls—from slow rollers and bunts to red-hot liners, such as the one the fielder is fielding at right.

Frequently, a baserunner advances to third base on an extra-base hit and must be tagged out. In the photographs below, notice that Kathy is straddling the bag at third base. She places the ball in her glove and covers it with her bare hand. She holds the ball down and in front of the base and lets the baserunner slide into the tag.

HITTING THE CUTOFF

Relays are used when the throw is beyond the range of an outfielder or it needs to move quickly. A ball can be returned to the infield more rapidly by two flat, short throws than by a single, high throw.

In the example shown above, a ball is hit to Colleen in centerfield. Molly, the shortstop, races to a spot in a straight line between the centerfielder and the catcher. Colleen fires the ball to Molly so that it reaches her at chest level. Molly catches the ball. She pivots backward on her ball-hand foot and quickly relays the ball to Tripper with no wasted motion.

OUTFIELD

Outfielders must possess speed, fielding ability, and a good arm. The centerfielder needs the most speed, since that territory is largest. The leftfielder needs to be prepared for hard shots down the third base line. The rightfielder must have a strong arm to throw the ball to third base.

Outfielders can improve their team's defense by backing up their teammates. Even when the ball doesn't make it into the outfield, the outfielders should know which base to back up on each play in case of a bad throw. For example, rightfielders can back up every throw to first base.

Another way to stay alert is for the outfielders to pay attention to each batter and adjust their position depending on whether the batter is right- or left-handed. They should also consider the batter's size, stance, and where he or she hit the ball the last time.

PLAYING THE GAME

To give you an idea of how these skills are used in a game, we'll follow the Maroons and the Golds as these rivals enter the seventh and final inning of their game. The Maroons are ahead 6-5.

Before the last inning starts, Katie catches Leah's final practice pitch and fires it to Allison at second base. Katie yells "Three up. Three down."

The first Golds batter walks toward the plate. She takes two final practice swings before stepping into the batter's box. Leah gets the signal from Katie. Her arm rotates up and back in the windmill.

The ball slaps into Katie's mitt. The umpire lifts his left hand. Ball one. Leah catches the ball from Katie and delivers another pitch. The Golds batter swings. The ball spins over the bat and high into the air. Katie rips the mask off her face so she can find the ball more easily. She spots it coming down to her right and tosses her mask to the left so she won't trip over it. Her bare hand follows the ball into her mitt. One out.

Dorothy, the next Golds batter, steps up to the plate. Katie signals a rise ball. Leah delivers it. Dorothy swings where she thought the ball would be—at chest level. The pitch whizzes past her shoulders. "Strike!" the umpire announces.

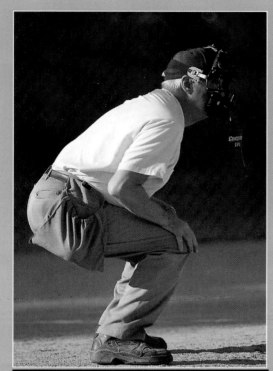

BEHIND THE PLATE

Umpires enforce the rules of the game. Like the catcher, the home plate umpire wears a face mask and chest protector. The home plate umpire calls balls and strikes and decides whether the ball is fair or foul. The base umpires rule on whether a batter is safe or out and whether an outfielder has caught a ball before it touched the ground.

On the next pitch, Dorothy drives a hard ground ball up the middle. The centerfielder charges the ball and sidearms it to Allison at second base. Dorothy rounds first base, but quickly retreats to the bag.

As Anne leaves the **on-deck circle,** the Maroons on first and third take a couple of steps forward. Not only is it a sacrifice bunt situation, but Anne laid down a picture-perfect drag bunt for a single earlier in the game. As Leah begins her delivery, Anne shifts into the bunting stance facing the pitcher. The fielders at first and third charge toward the plate while Allison covers first base.

Anne directs the ball into the dirt up the third base line. The fielder playing third base allows the ball to dribble over the white chalk line. "Foul ball!" the umpire roars.

Anne walks back to the plate and picks up her bat. Leah burns in another inside pitch. Instead of bunting, Anne drives a blistering line drive just inside the third base line. Dorothy scores. The third base coach sends Anne home. Anne slides under the catcher's mitt. The umpire signals "Safe."

Katie hands the ball to Leah, who had backed up the play at home. "Shake it off," Katie tells Leah. "Get the next two batters."

Leah maintains her composure. The next two Golds batters ground out to the shortstop. Katie dashes to the dugout to take off her chest protector and shin guards. She'll be the first batter for the Maroons.

"Start us off, Katie," Leah calls as she pulls on a jacket. Katie grins at her friend from the on-deck circle. When Katie steps into the batter's box, she keeps her eyes fixed on the ball all the way in until she stares down the barrel of her bat. The ball flies over the backstop.

The second pitch looks high and outside, but the umpire calls another strike. Katie steps out of the box and takes a practice swing. She steps in and taps a blooper over the shortstop's head. The ball drops neatly into the hole between the infield and outfield for a single.

Mary follows her teammate's performance by driving one up the middle. Dorothy charges the ball but it bounces over her glove. The ball caroms off Dorothy's leg and rolls several feet away. The leftfielder, who was backing up her teammate, makes the stop. The third base coach holds up Katie at third. Mary has a stand-up double.

The Golds pitcher walks the next batter, loading the bases. Then Leah steps up to the plate. She raps a hard fly ball into the hole between the rightfielder and centerfielder. The runner on first starts for second, confident that the ball won't be caught, but Dorothy makes a diving

catch. She rolls to her feet and throws the ball to first base. The ball beats the runner back to first. Double play! But Katie had tagged up at third and scores to tie the game.

Leah walks back to her dugout and finds a spot next to Katie on the bench. "Don't worry," Katie tells Leah. "We have Mary in scoring position."

Leah and Katie leap to their feet as Mary goes to third on a **wild pitch.** "Get a little hit, Diane,'" Molly calls as the next batter approaches the plate. "I want to go home." But Diane quickly gets two strikes against her.

With nerves of steel she lets the next two balls go by. Then she drives a hard liner between second and third. The fielder at third leaps to make the catch but the ball bounces off her glove into short leftfield. The leftfielder bare-hands the ball and fires it to first. Thud. Slap. Diane beats the throw by a split second. Mary scores. The Maroons win the game!

Diane and Mary lead their team to the center of the field to shake hands with the other team.

SOFTBALL TALK

ball: A pitch that doesn't pass through the strike zone and at which the batter doesn't swing.

batting order: The order in which players bat. Players may not bat out of order, but substitutions are allowed.

bunt: A softly hit ball.

count: The number of balls and strikes against a batter. The number of balls is always given first. If the umpire has called two strikes and three balls, the count is 3-and-2, or three balls and two strikes.

drag bunt: A bunt that a batter disguises until the last possible moment. A drag bunt is used when the batter is trying to reach base safely.

extra-base hit: A hit that allows the batter to advance past first base. A double gets the batter to second base, a triple to third, and a home run to home plate.

fly ball: A ball that is hit high into the air in fair territory.

force-out: A situation in which a baserunner must go to the next base, but the fielder holding the ball touches the base before the runner. A force-out, also called a force play, can only happen at first base or when all the bases behind the runner are occupied.

foul ball: A batted ball that lands outside the foul lines.

ground ball: A batted ball that rolls on the ground. Also called a grounder.

line drive: A hard-hit ball that travels on a straight, relatively low path.

on-deck circle: The area, often outlined with chalk, where the next batter in the order waits.

opposite field: Rightfield for a right-handed batter and leftfield for a left-handed batter.

out: The failure of a batter or runner to reach a base safely. A team is allowed three outs in an inning.

pitching rubber: The rectangle set in the middle of the infield where the pitcher must stand when delivering the ball.

pull the ball: Hitting the ball to leftfield for a righthanded batter and rightfield for a lefthander.

sacrifice bunt: A play in which the batter bunts and is put out but succeeds in moving a teammate at least one base. The batter's team must have fewer than two outs.

scoring position: A baserunner on second or third base is in scoring position.

strike: A pitch that passes through the strike zone without being hit. Also, a pitch that is hit foul when the batter has fewer than two strikes.

strikeout: An out that results from the batter being charged with three strikes.

strike zone: The invisible area over home plate through which the pitch must pass to be called a strike.

tag: An out a fielder makes by touching a runner with the ball.

tag up: The act of touching one's original base, after a fielder catches a fly ball, in order to be able to go to the next base.

walk: A free pass to first base, awarded to a batter who takes four balls without being put out by a strikeout or a fielder. Also called a base on balls.

wild pitch: A pitch well outside the strike zone that is difficult for the catcher to block or catch.

FURTHER READING

Kneer, Marian E. and Charles L. McCord. *Softball: Slow and Fast Pitch.* Dubuque, Iowa: Brown & Benchmark, 1995.

Monteleone, John and Deborah Crisfield. *The Louisville Slugger Complete Book of Women's Fast-Pitch Softball.* New York, New York: Henry Holt & Co., 1999.

Pagnoni, Mario and Gerald Robinson. *Softball: Fast and Slow Pitch.* Indianapolis, Indiana: Masters Press, 1995.

Richardson, Dot and Don Yaeger. *Living the Dream.* New York, New York: Kensington Publishing, 1997.

Sammons, Barry and Lisa Fernandez. *Fastpitch Softball: The Windmill Pitcher.* Indianapolis, Indiana: Masters Press, 1998.

FOR MORE INFORMATION

Amateur Softball Association
2801 N.E. 50th Street
Oklahoma City, OK 73111
www.softball.org

American Fastpitch Association
2536 Greenacre Avenue
Anaheim, CA 92801
www. afasoftball.com

INDEX